replenish

to fill up again.

180 day
self-care
daily-planner

for the busy person
looking to crush their goals and fill their self-care tank.

Created By: Josefina H. Sanders of Love Offering

i am allowed to rest without guilt and replenish without shame.

JOSEFINA H. SANDERS

Wind Down:

i am thankful for		

night routine	celebrating myself tonight for	tomorrow's tasks
☐		☐
☐		☐
☐		☐
☐		☐
☐		☐
		☐
i will decompress by:		☐
		☐

ending on a good note
3 good things that happened today

Wind Up:

word of the day		date

morning routine	goal for today	tasks
☐		☐
☐		☐
☐		☐
☐		☐
☐		☐
		☐
i will practice self-care by:		☐
		☐

brain dump

what's on your mind?

_____

_____

_____

_____

_____

_____

_____

_____

_____

_____

_____

Wind Down:

i am thankful for

night routine	celebrating myself tonight for	tomorrow's tasks
☐		☐
☐		☐
☐		☐
☐		☐
☐		☐
		☐

i will decompress by:

☐
☐
☐

ending on a good note

3 good things that happened today

_____
_____
_____
_____
_____
_____
_____
_____
_____
_____

Wind Up:

word of the day	date

morning routine	goal for today	tasks
☐		☐
☐		☐
☐		☐
☐		☐
☐		☐
		☐
i will practice self-care by:		☐
		☐

brain dump
what's on your mind?

Wind Down:

i am thankful for

night routine	celebrating myself tonight for	tomorrow's tasks
☐		☐
☐		☐
☐		☐
☐		☐
☐		☐
		☐
i will decompress by:		☐
		☐

ending on a good note

3 good things that happened today

Wind Up:

word of the day		date

morning routine	goal for today	tasks
☐		☐
☐		☐
☐		☐
☐		☐
☐		☐
		☐
i will practice self-care by:		☐
		☐

brain dump
what's on your mind?

_____

_____

_____

_____

_____

_____

_____

_____

_____

_____

_____

_____

_____

_____

Wind Down:

i am thankful for

<table>
<tr><td colspan="2">night routine</td><td>celebrating myself tonight for</td><td>tomorrow's tasks</td></tr>
<tr><td>☐</td><td></td><td></td><td>☐</td></tr>
<tr><td>☐</td><td></td><td></td><td>☐</td></tr>
<tr><td>☐</td><td></td><td></td><td>☐</td></tr>
<tr><td>☐</td><td></td><td></td><td>☐</td></tr>
<tr><td>☐</td><td></td><td></td><td>☐</td></tr>
<tr><td colspan="2">i will decompress by:</td><td></td><td>☐
☐
☐</td></tr>
</table>

ending on a good note

3 good things that happened today

Wind Up:

word of the day	date

morning routine	goal for today	tasks
☐		☐
☐		☐
☐		☐
☐		☐
☐		☐

i will practice self-care by:	☐
	☐
	☐

brain dump
what's on your mind?

Wind Down:

i am thankful for

night routine	celebrating myself tonight for	tomorrow's tasks
☐		☐
☐		☐
☐		☐
☐		☐
☐		☐
		☐
i will decompress by:		☐
		☐

ending on a good note

3 good things that happened today

Wind Up:

word of the day		date

morning routine	goal for today	tasks
☐		☐
☐		☐
☐		☐
☐		☐
☐		☐
i will practice self-care by:		☐
		☐
		☐

brain dump

what's on your mind?

_____

_____

_____

_____

_____

_____

_____

_____

_____

_____

_____

Wind Down:

i am thankful for

night routine	celebrating myself tonight for	tomorrow's tasks
☐		☐
☐		☐
☐		☐
☐		☐
☐		☐
		☐
i will decompress by:		☐
		☐

ending on a good note
3 good things that happened today

Wind Up:

word of the day		date

morning routine	goal for today	tasks
☐		☐
☐		☐
☐		☐
☐		☐
☐		☐
		☐
i will practice self-care by:		☐
		☐

brain dump

what's on your mind?

Wind Down:

i am thankful for

night routine	**celebrating myself tonight for**	**tomorrow's tasks**
☐		☐
☐		☐
☐		☐
☐		☐
☐		☐
		☐
i will decompress by:		☐
		☐

ending on a good note

3 good things that happened today

Wind Up:

word of the day		date

morning routine	goal for today	tasks
☐		☐
☐		☐
☐		☐
☐		☐
☐		☐
		☐
i will practice self-care by:		☐
		☐

brain dump
what's on your mind?

Wind Down:

i am thankful for

night routine	celebrating myself tonight for	tomorrow's tasks
☐		☐
☐		☐
☐		☐
☐		☐
☐		☐
		☐
i will decompress by:		☐
		☐

ending on a good note

3 good things that happened today

_____

_____

_____

_____

_____

_____

_____

_____

_____

_____

_____

Wind Up:

word of the day	date

morning routine	goal for today	tasks
☐		☐
☐		☐
☐		☐
☐		☐
☐		☐
		☐
i will practice self-care by:		☐
		☐

brain dump

what's on your mind?

Wind Down:

i am thankful for

night routine	celebrating myself tonight for	tomorrow's tasks
☐		☐
☐		☐
☐		☐
☐		☐
☐		☐
		☐
i will decompress by:		☐
		☐

ending on a good note

3 good things that happened today

Wind Up:

word of the day	date

morning routine	goal for today	tasks
☐		☐
☐		☐
☐		☐
☐		☐
☐		☐
		☐
i will practice self-care by:		☐
		☐

brain dump
what's on your mind?

Wind Down:

i am thankful for

.

night routine	celebrating myself tonight for	tomorrow's tasks
☐		☐
☐		☐
☐		☐
☐		☐
☐		☐
		☐
i will decompress by:		☐
		☐

ending on a good note

3 good things that happened today

Wind Up:

word of the day	date

morning routine	goal for today	tasks
☐		☐
☐		☐
☐		☐
☐		☐
☐		☐
		☐
i will practice self-care by:		☐
		☐

brain dump

what's on your mind?

Wind Down:

i am thankful for

night routine	celebrating myself tonight for	tomorrow's tasks
☐		☐
☐		☐
☐		☐
☐		☐
☐		☐
		☐
i will decompress by:		☐
		☐

ending on a good note

3 good things that happened today

Wind Up:

word of the day	date

morning routine	goal for today	tasks
☐		☐
☐		☐
☐		☐
☐		☐
☐		☐
		☐
i will practice self-care by:		☐
		☐

brain dump
what's on your mind?

Wind Down:

i am thankful for

night routine	celebrating myself tonight for	tomorrow's tasks
☐		☐
☐		☐
☐		☐
☐		☐
☐		☐
		☐

i will decompress by:

☐
☐
☐

ending on a good note

3 good things that happened today

Wind Up:

word of the day	date

morning routine	goal for today	tasks
☐		☐
☐		☐
☐		☐
☐		☐
☐		☐
		☐
i will practice self-care by:		☐
		☐

brain dump

what's on your mind?

Wind Down:

i am thankful for

night routine	celebrating myself tonight for	tomorrow's tasks
☐		☐
☐		☐
☐		☐
☐		☐
☐		☐
		☐
i will decompress by:		☐
		☐

ending on a good note
3 good things that happened today

Wind Up:

word of the day		date

morning routine	goal for today	tasks
☐		☐
☐		☐
☐		☐
☐		☐
☐		☐
		☐
i will practice self-care by:		☐
		☐

brain dump

what's on your mind?

Wind Down:

i am thankful for

night routine	celebrating myself tonight for	tomorrow's tasks
☐		☐
☐		☐
☐		☐
☐		☐
☐		☐
		☐
i will decompress by:		☐
		☐

ending on a good note

3 good things that happened today

Wind Up:

word of the day	date

morning routine	goal for today	tasks
☐		☐
☐		☐
☐		☐
☐		☐
☐		☐
		☐
i will practice self-care by:		☐
		☐

brain dump

what's on your mind?

Wind Down:

i am thankful for

night routine	celebrating myself tonight for	tomorrow's tasks
☐		☐
☐		☐
☐		☐
☐		☐
☐		☐
		☐
i will decompress by:		☐
		☐

ending on a good note

3 good things that happened today

_____

_____

_____

_____

_____

_____

_____

_____

_____

_____

Wind Up:

word of the day	date

morning routine	goal for today	tasks
☐		☐
☐		☐
☐		☐
☐		☐
☐		☐
		☐
i will practice self-care by:		☐
		☐

brain dump
what's on your mind?

_____

_____

_____

_____

_____

_____

_____

_____

_____

_____

Wind Down:

i am thankful for

night routine	celebrating myself tonight for	tomorrow's tasks
☐		☐
☐		☐
☐		☐
☐		☐
☐		☐
		☐
i will decompress by:		☐
		☐

ending on a good note

3 good things that happened today

Wind Up:

word of the day	date

morning routine	goal for today	tasks
☐		☐
☐		☐
☐		☐
☐		☐
☐		☐
		☐
i will practice self-care by:		☐
		☐

brain dump

what's on your mind?

Wind Down:

i am thankful for

night routine	celebrating myself tonight for	tomorrow's tasks
☐		☐
☐		☐
☐		☐
☐		☐
☐		☐
		☐
i will decompress by:		☐
		☐

ending on a good note

3 good things that happened today

Wind Up:

word of the day		date

morning routine	goal for today	tasks
☐		☐
☐		☐
☐		☐
☐		☐
☐		☐
		☐
i will practice self-care by:		☐
		☐

brain dump

what's on your mind?

Wind Down:

i am thankful for

night routine	celebrating myself tonight for	tomorrow's tasks
☐		☐
☐		☐
☐		☐
☐		☐
☐		☐
		☐
i will decompress by:		☐
		☐

ending on a good note

3 good things that happened today

_____

_____

_____

_____

_____

_____

_____

_____

_____

_____

Wind Up:

word of the day		date

morning routine	goal for today	tasks
☐		☐
☐		☐
☐		☐
☐		☐
☐		☐
		☐
i will practice self-care by:		☐
		☐

brain dump

what's on your mind?

_____

_____

_____

_____

_____

_____

_____

_____

_____

_____

_____

Wind Down:

i am thankful for

night routine	celebrating myself tonight for	tomorrow's tasks
☐		☐
☐		☐
☐		☐
☐		☐
☐		☐
		☐
i will decompress by:		☐
		☐

ending on a good note

3 good things that happened today

Wind Up:

word of the day		date
morning routine	goal for today	tasks

morning routine
☐
☐
☐
☐
☐

goal for today

tasks
☐
☐
☐
☐
☐
☐
☐
☐

i will practice self-care by:

brain dump

what's on your mind?

Wind Down:

i am thankful for

night routine	celebrating myself tonight for	tomorrow's tasks
☐		☐
☐		☐
☐		☐
☐		☐
☐		☐
		☐
i will decompress by:		☐
		☐

ending on a good note
3 good things that happened today

Wind Up:

word of the day		date
morning routine	goal for today	tasks
☐		☐
☐		☐
☐		☐
☐		☐
☐		☐
		☐
i will practice self-care by:		☐
		☐

brain dump
what's on your mind?

Wind Down:

i am thankful for

night routine	celebrating myself tonight for	tomorrow's tasks
☐		☐
☐		☐
☐		☐
☐		☐
☐		☐
		☐
i will decompress by:		☐
		☐

ending on a good note
3 good things that happened today

_____

_____

_____

_____

_____

_____

_____

_____

_____

Wind Up:

word of the day		date

morning routine	goal for today	tasks
☐		☐
☐		☐
☐		☐
☐		☐
☐		☐
		☐
i will practice self-care by:		☐
		☐

brain dump

what's on your mind?

Wind Down:

i am thankful for

night routine	celebrating myself tonight for	tomorrow's tasks
☐		☐
☐		☐
☐		☐
☐		☐
☐		☐
		☐
i will decompress by:		☐
		☐

ending on a good note
3 good things that happened today

Wind Up:

word of the day	date

morning routine	goal for today	tasks
☐		☐
☐		☐
☐		☐
☐		☐
☐		☐
		☐
i will practice self-care by:		☐
		☐

brain dump

what's on your mind?

Wind Down:

i am thankful for

night routine	celebrating myself tonight for	tomorrow's tasks
☐		☐
☐		☐
☐		☐
☐		☐
☐		☐
		☐

i will decompress by:

☐
☐
☐

ending on a good note

3 good things that happened today

Wind Up:

word of the day	date

morning routine	goal for today	tasks
☐		☐
☐		☐
☐		☐
☐		☐
☐		☐
		☐
i will practice self-care by:		☐
		☐

brain dump

what's on your mind?

Wind Down:

i am thankful for

night routine	celebrating myself tonight for	tomorrow's tasks
☐		☐
☐		☐
☐		☐
☐		☐
☐		☐
		☐

i will decompress by:

☐
☐
☐

ending on a good note
3 good things that happened today

_____

_____

_____

_____

_____

_____

_____

_____

_____

_____

Wind Up:

word of the day		date

morning routine	goal for today	tasks
☐		☐
☐		☐
☐		☐
☐		☐
☐		☐
		☐
i will practice self-care by:		☐
		☐

brain dump

what's on your mind?

_____

_____

_____

_____

_____

_____

_____

_____

_____

_____

_____

_____

_____

_____

Wind Down:

i am thankful for

night routine	celebrating myself tonight for	tomorrow's tasks
☐		☐
☐		☐
☐		☐
☐		☐
☐		☐
		☐
i will decompress by:		☐
		☐

ending on a good note

3 good things that happened today

Wind Up:

word of the day		date

morning routine	goal for today	tasks
☐		☐
☐		☐
☐		☐
☐		☐
☐		☐
		☐
i will practice self-care by:		☐
		☐

brain dump

what's on your mind?

Wind Down:

i am thankful for

night routine	celebrating myself tonight for	tomorrow's tasks
☐		☐
☐		☐
☐		☐
☐		☐
☐		☐
		☐
i will decompress by:		☐
		☐

ending on a good note

3 good things that happened today

Wind Up:

word of the day		date

morning routine	goal for today	tasks
☐		☐
☐		☐
☐		☐
☐		☐
☐		☐
		☐
i will practice self-care by:		☐
		☐

brain dump

what's on your mind?

Wind Down:

i am thankful for		
night routine	celebrating myself tonight for	tomorrow's tasks
☐ ☐ ☐ ☐ ☐		☐ ☐ ☐ ☐ ☐ ☐ ☐ ☐
i will decompress by:		

ending on a good note

3 good things that happened today

Wind Up:

word of the day	date

morning routine	goal for today	tasks
☐		☐
☐		☐
☐		☐
☐		☐
☐		☐
		☐
i will practice self-care by:		☐
		☐

brain dump

what's on your mind?

Wind Down:

i am thankful for

night routine	celebrating myself tonight for	tomorrow's tasks
☐		☐
☐		☐
☐		☐
☐		☐
☐		☐
		☐
i will decompress by:		☐
		☐

ending on a good note

3 good things that happened today

_____
_____
_____
_____
_____
_____
_____
_____
_____
_____

Wind Up:

word of the day	date

morning routine	goal for today	tasks
☐		☐
☐		☐
☐		☐
☐		☐
☐		☐
		☐
i will practice self-care by:		☐
		☐

brain dump

what's on your mind?

Wind Down:

i am thankful for

.

night routine	celebrating myself tonight for	tomorrow's tasks
☐		☐
☐		☐
☐		☐
☐		☐
☐		☐
		☐
i will decompress by:		☐
		☐

ending on a good note

3 good things that happened today

_____
_____
_____
_____
_____
_____
_____
_____
_____
_____

Wind Up:

word of the day		date

morning routine	goal for today	tasks
☐		☐
☐		☐
☐		☐
☐		☐
☐		☐
		☐
i will practice self-care by:		☐
		☐

brain dump

what's on your mind?

Wind Down:

i am thankful for

night routine	celebrating myself tonight for	tomorrow's tasks
☐		☐
☐		☐
☐		☐
☐		☐
☐		☐
		☐
i will decompress by:		☐
		☐

ending on a good note

3 good things that happened today

Wind Up:

word of the day		date

morning routine	goal for today	tasks
☐		☐
☐		☐
☐		☐
☐		☐
☐		☐
		☐
i will practice self-care by:		☐
		☐

brain dump

what's on your mind?

Wind Down:

i am thankful for		

night routine	celebrating myself tonight for	tomorrow's tasks
☐		☐
☐		☐
☐		☐
☐		☐
☐		☐
i will decompress by:		☐
		☐
		☐

ending on a good note

3 good things that happened today

_____

_____

_____

_____

_____

_____

_____

_____

_____

Wind Up:

word of the day		date

morning routine	goal for today	tasks
☐		☐
☐		☐
☐		☐
☐		☐
☐		☐
		☐
i will practice self-care by:		☐
		☐

brain dump

what's on your mind?

Wind Down:

i am thankful for

night routine	celebrating myself tonight for	tomorrow's tasks
☐		☐
☐		☐
☐		☐
☐		☐
☐		☐
		☐
i will decompress by:		☐
		☐

ending on a good note

3 good things that happened today

_____

_____

_____

_____

_____

_____

_____

_____

_____

_____

_____

Wind Up:

word of the day		date

morning routine	goal for today	tasks
☐		☐
☐		☐
☐		☐
☐		☐
☐		☐
		☐
i will practice self-care by:		☐
		☐

brain dump

what's on your mind?

Wind Down:

i am thankful for

night routine	celebrating myself tonight for	tomorrow's tasks
☐		☐
☐		☐
☐		☐
☐		☐
☐		☐
		☐
i will decompress by:		☐
		☐

ending on a good note

3 good things that happened today

Wind Up:

word of the day		date

morning routine	goal for today	tasks
☐		☐
☐		☐
☐		☐
☐		☐
☐		☐
		☐
i will practice self-care by:		☐
		☐

brain dump

what's on your mind?

Wind Down:

i am thankful for

night routine	celebrating myself tonight for	tomorrow's tasks
☐		☐
☐		☐
☐		☐
☐		☐
☐		☐
		☐
i will decompress by:		☐
		☐

ending on a good note

3 good things that happened today

Wind Up:

word of the day		date

morning routine	goal for today	tasks
☐		☐
☐		☐
☐		☐
☐		☐
☐		☐
		☐
i will practice self-care by:		☐
		☐

brain dump

what's on your mind?

_____

_____

_____

_____

_____

_____

_____

_____

_____

_____

_____

_____

_____

Wind Down:

i am thankful for

night routine	celebrating myself tonight for	tomorrow's tasks
☐		☐
☐		☐
☐		☐
☐		☐
☐		☐
		☐

i will decompress by:

☐
☐
☐

ending on a good note

3 good things that happened today

_____

_____

_____

_____

_____

_____

_____

_____

_____

_____

Wind Up:

word of the day		date
morning routine	goal for today	tasks

morning routine
- [ ]
- [ ]
- [ ]
- [ ]
- [ ]

goal for today

tasks
- [ ]
- [ ]
- [ ]
- [ ]
- [ ]
- [ ]
- [ ]
- [ ]

i will practice self-care by:

brain dump
what's on your mind?

Wind Down:

i am thankful for

night routine	celebrating myself tonight for	tomorrow's tasks
☐		☐
☐		☐
☐		☐
☐		☐
☐		☐
		☐

i will decompress by:

☐
☐

ending on a good note

3 good things that happened today

Wind Up:

word of the day		date

morning routine	goal for today	tasks
☐		☐
☐		☐
☐		☐
☐		☐
☐		☐
		☐
i will practice self-care by:		☐
		☐

brain dump

what's on your mind?

Wind Down:

i am thankful for

night routine	celebrating myself tonight for	tomorrow's tasks
☐		☐
☐		☐
☐		☐
☐		☐
☐		☐
		☐
i will decompress by:		☐
		☐

ending on a good note

3 good things that happened today

Wind Up:

word of the day		date

morning routine	goal for today	tasks
☐		☐
☐		☐
☐		☐
☐		☐
☐		☐
		☐
i will practice self-care by:		☐
		☐

brain dump

what's on your mind?

_____

_____

_____

_____

_____

_____

_____

_____

_____

_____

Wind Down:

i am thankful for

night routine

☐
☐
☐
☐
☐

celebrating myself tonight for

tomorrow's tasks

☐
☐
☐
☐
☐
☐
☐
☐

i will decompress by:

ending on a good note

3 good things that happened today

Wind Up:

word of the day	date

morning routine	goal for today	tasks
☐		☐
☐		☐
☐		☐
☐		☐
☐		☐
		☐
i will practice self-care by:		☐
		☐

brain dump
what's on your mind?

Wind Down:

i am thankful for

night routine	celebrating myself tonight for	tomorrow's tasks
☐		☐
☐		☐
☐		☐
☐		☐
☐		☐
		☐
i will decompress by:		☐
		☐

ending on a good note

3 good things that happened today

Wind Up:

word of the day	date

morning routine	goal for today	tasks
☐		☐
☐		☐
☐		☐
☐		☐
☐		☐
		☐
i will practice self-care by:		☐
		☐

brain dump

what's on your mind?

_____

_____

_____

_____

_____

_____

_____

_____

_____

_____

_____

_____

Wind Down:

i am thankful for

	night routine	celebrating myself tonight for	tomorrow's tasks
☐			☐
☐			☐
☐			☐
☐			☐
☐			☐

i will decompress by:

☐
☐
☐
☐

ending on a good note

3 good things that happened today

_____

_____

_____

_____

_____

_____

_____

_____

_____

Wind Up:

word of the day		date
morning routine	goal for today	tasks

morning routine
- [ ]
- [ ]
- [ ]
- [ ]
- [ ]

i will practice self-care by:

tasks
- [ ]
- [ ]
- [ ]
- [ ]
- [ ]
- [ ]
- [ ]
- [ ]

brain dump

what's on your mind?

Wind Down:

i am thankful for

night routine	celebrating myself tonight for	tomorrow's tasks
☐		☐
☐		☐
☐		☐
☐		☐
☐		☐
		☐
i will decompress by:		☐
		☐

ending on a good note

3 good things that happened today

Wind Up:

word of the day	date

morning routine	goal for today	tasks
☐		☐
☐		☐
☐		☐
☐		☐
☐		☐
		☐
i will practice self-care by:		☐
		☐

brain dump

what's on your mind?

_____

_____

_____

_____

_____

_____

_____

_____

_____

_____

Wind Down:

i am thankful for

night routine	celebrating myself tonight for	tomorrow's tasks
☐		☐
☐		☐
☐		☐
☐		☐
☐		☐
		☐
i will decompress by:		☐
		☐

ending on a good note

3 good things that happened today

Wind Up:

word of the day		date

morning routine	goal for today	tasks
☐		☐
☐		☐
☐		☐
☐		☐
☐		☐
		☐
i will practice self-care by:		☐
		☐

brain dump

what's on your mind?

Wind Down:

i am thankful for

night routine	celebrating myself tonight for	tomorrow's tasks
☐		☐
☐		☐
☐		☐
☐		☐
☐		☐
		☐

i will decompress by:

☐
☐
☐

ending on a good note

3 good things that happened today

_____

_____

_____

_____

_____

_____

_____

_____

_____

_____

Wind Up:

word of the day		date

morning routine	goal for today	tasks
☐		☐
☐		☐
☐		☐
☐		☐
☐		☐
i will practice self-care by:		☐
		☐
		☐

brain dump

what's on your mind?

_____

_____

_____

_____

_____

_____

_____

_____

_____

_____

Wind Down:

i am thankful for

night routine	celebrating myself tonight for	tomorrow's tasks
☐		☐
☐		☐
☐		☐
☐		☐
☐		☐
		☐
i will decompress by:		☐
		☐
		☐

ending on a good note

3 good things that happened today

Wind Up:

word of the day	date

morning routine	goal for today	tasks
☐		☐
☐		☐
☐		☐
☐		☐
☐		☐
		☐
i will practice self-care by:		☐
		☐

brain dump

what's on your mind?

Wind Down:

i am thankful for

night routine	celebrating myself tonight for	tomorrow's tasks
☐		☐
☐		☐
☐		☐
☐		☐
☐		☐

i will decompress by:

☐
☐
☐

ending on a good note
3 good things that happened today

_____

_____

_____

_____

_____

_____

_____

_____

_____

_____

_____

_____

_____

_____

Wind Up:

word of the day		date
morning routine	goal for today	tasks

morning routine
☐
☐
☐
☐
☐

i will practice self-care by:

tasks
☐
☐
☐
☐
☐
☐
☐
☐

brain dump
what's on your mind?

Wind Down:

i am thankful for

night routine	celebrating myself tonight for	tomorrow's tasks
☐		☐
☐		☐
☐		☐
☐		☐
☐		☐

i will decompress by:

☐
☐
☐

ending on a good note

3 good things that happened today

_____

_____

_____

_____

_____

_____

_____

_____

_____

Wind Up:

word of the day	date

morning routine	goal for today	tasks
☐		☐
☐		☐
☐		☐
☐		☐
☐		☐
		☐
i will practice self-care by:		☐
		☐

brain dump

what's on your mind?

_____

_____

_____

_____

_____

_____

_____

_____

_____

_____

_____

_____

_____

Wind Down:

i am thankful for

night routine	celebrating myself tonight for	tomorrow's tasks
☐		☐
☐		☐
☐		☐
☐		☐
☐		☐
		☐

i will decompress by:

☐
☐
☐

ending on a good note
3 good things that happened today

Wind Up:

word of the day	date

morning routine	goal for today	tasks
☐		☐
☐		☐
☐		☐
☐		☐
☐		☐
		☐
i will practice self-care by:		☐
		☐

brain dump

what's on your mind?

Wind Down:

i am thankful for

night routine	celebrating myself tonight for	tomorrow's tasks
☐		☐
☐		☐
☐		☐
☐		☐
☐		☐
		☐
i will decompress by:		☐
		☐

ending on a good note
3 good things that happened today

Wind Up:

word of the day	date

morning routine	goal for today	tasks
☐		☐
☐		☐
☐		☐
☐		☐
☐		☐
		☐
i will practice self-care by:		☐
		☐

brain dump
what's on your mind?

Wind Down:

i am thankful for

night routine	celebrating myself tonight for	tomorrow's tasks
☐		☐
☐		☐
☐		☐
☐		☐
☐		☐
		☐
i will decompress by:		☐
		☐

ending on a good note
3 good things that happened today

_____

_____

_____

_____

_____

_____

_____

_____

_____

_____

Wind Up:

word of the day	date

morning routine	goal for today	tasks
☐		☐
☐		☐
☐		☐
☐		☐
☐		☐
		☐
i will practice self-care by:		☐
		☐

brain dump

what's on your mind?

Wind Down:

i am thankful for

night routine	celebrating myself tonight for	tomorrow's tasks
☐		☐
☐		☐
☐		☐
☐		☐
☐		☐
		☐
i will decompress by:		☐
		☐

ending on a good note

3 good things that happened today

Wind Up:

word of the day	date

morning routine	goal for today	tasks
☐		☐
☐		☐
☐		☐
☐		☐
☐		☐
		☐
i will practice self-care by:		☐
		☐

brain dump
what's on your mind?

Wind Down:

i am thankful for

night routine	celebrating myself tonight for	tomorrow's tasks
☐		☐
☐		☐
☐		☐
☐		☐
☐		☐

i will decompress by:

☐
☐
☐

ending on a good note

3 good things that happened today

Wind Up:

word of the day	date

morning routine	goal for today	tasks
☐		☐
☐		☐
☐		☐
☐		☐
☐		☐
		☐
i will practice self-care by:		☐
		☐

brain dump

what's on your mind?

_____

_____

_____

_____

_____

_____

_____

_____

_____

_____

_____

Wind Down:

i am thankful for

night routine	celebrating myself tonight for	tomorrow's tasks
☐		☐
☐		☐
☐		☐
☐		☐
☐		☐
		☐
i will decompress by:		☐
		☐

ending on a good note

3 good things that happened today

Wind Up:

word of the day		date

morning routine	goal for today	tasks
☐		☐
☐		☐
☐		☐
☐		☐
☐		☐
		☐
i will practice self-care by:		☐
		☐

brain dump

what's on your mind?

Wind Down:

i am thankful for

night routine	celebrating myself tonight for	tomorrow's tasks
☐		☐
☐		☐
☐		☐
☐		☐
☐		☐
		☐
i will decompress by:		☐
		☐

ending on a good note

3 good things that happened today

Wind Up:

word of the day		date

morning routine	goal for today	tasks
☐		☐
☐		☐
☐		☐
☐		☐
☐		☐
		☐
i will practice self-care by:		☐
		☐

brain dump

what's on your mind?

Wind Down:

i am thankful for

night routine	celebrating myself tonight for	tomorrow's tasks
☐		☐
☐		☐
☐		☐
☐		☐
☐		☐
		☐

i will decompress by:

☐
☐
☐

ending on a good note
3 good things that happened today

_____

_____

_____

_____

_____

_____

_____

_____

_____

_____

_____

Wind Up:

word of the day	date

morning routine	goal for today	tasks
☐		☐
☐		☐
☐		☐
☐		☐
☐		☐
		☐
i will practice self-care by:		☐
		☐

brain dump
what's on your mind?

_____

_____

_____

_____

_____

_____

_____

_____

_____

Wind Down:

i am thankful for

night routine

☐
☐
☐
☐
☐

celebrating myself tonight for

tomorrow's tasks

☐
☐
☐
☐
☐
☐
☐
☐

i will decompress by:

ending on a good note

3 good things that happened today

Wind Up:

word of the day	date

morning routine	goal for today	tasks
☐		☐
☐		☐
☐		☐
☐		☐
☐		☐
		☐
i will practice self-care by:		☐
		☐

brain dump

what's on your mind?

_____

_____

_____

_____

_____

_____

_____

_____

_____

_____

Wind Down:

i am thankful for

night routine	celebrating myself tonight for	tomorrow's tasks
☐		☐
☐		☐
☐		☐
☐		☐
☐		☐
		☐
i will decompress by:		☐
		☐

ending on a good note

3 good things that happened today

_____

_____

_____

_____

_____

_____

_____

_____

_____

_____

_____

Wind Up:

word of the day		date

morning routine	goal for today	tasks
☐		☐
☐		☐
☐		☐
☐		☐
☐		☐
		☐
i will practice self-care by:		☐
		☐

brain dump

what's on your mind?

_____

_____

_____

_____

_____

_____

_____

_____

_____

_____

_____

_____

_____

Wind Down:

i am thankful for

night routine	celebrating myself tonight for	tomorrow's tasks
☐		☐
☐		☐
☐		☐
☐		☐
☐		☐
		☐
i will decompress by:		☐
		☐

ending on a good note

3 good things that happened today

Wind Up:

word of the day		date

morning routine	goal for today	tasks
☐		☐
☐		☐
☐		☐
☐		☐
☐		☐
		☐
i will practice self-care by:		☐
		☐

brain dump

what's on your mind?

Wind Down:

i am thankful for

night routine	celebrating myself tonight for	tomorrow's tasks
☐		☐
☐		☐
☐		☐
☐		☐
☐		☐
		☐
i will decompress by:		☐
		☐
		☐

ending on a good note
3 good things that happened today

Wind Up:

word of the day	date

morning routine	goal for today	tasks
☐		☐
☐		☐
☐		☐
☐		☐
☐		☐
		☐
i will practice self-care by:		☐
		☐

brain dump

what's on your mind?

Wind Down:

i am thankful for

night routine	celebrating myself tonight for	tomorrow's tasks
☐		☐
☐		☐
☐		☐
☐		☐
☐		☐
		☐
i will decompress by:		☐
		☐

ending on a good note
3 good things that happened today

Wind Up:

word of the day		date
morning routine	goal for today	tasks
☐		☐
☐		☐
☐		☐
☐		☐
☐		☐
		☐
i will practice self-care by:		☐
		☐

brain dump

what's on your mind?

_____

_____

_____

_____

_____

_____

_____

_____

_____

_____

Wind Down:

i am thankful for

night routine	celebrating myself tonight for	tomorrow's tasks
☐		☐
☐		☐
☐		☐
☐		☐
☐		☐
		☐
i will decompress by:		☐
		☐

ending on a good note

3 good things that happened today

Wind Up:

word of the day		date

morning routine	goal for today	tasks
☐		☐
☐		☐
☐		☐
☐		☐
☐		☐
		☐
i will practice self-care by:		☐
		☐

brain dump

what's on your mind?

Wind Down:

i am thankful for

night routine	celebrating myself tonight for	tomorrow's tasks
☐		☐
☐		☐
☐		☐
☐		☐
☐		☐

i will decompress by:

☐
☐
☐

ending on a good note

3 good things that happened today

_____

_____

_____

_____

_____

_____

_____

_____

_____

Wind Up:

word of the day		date

morning routine	goal for today	tasks
☐		☐
☐		☐
☐		☐
☐		☐
☐		☐
		☐
i will practice self-care by:		☐
		☐

brain dump

what's on your mind?

Wind Down:

i am thankful for

night routine	celebrating myself tonight for	tomorrow's tasks
☐		☐
☐		☐
☐		☐
☐		☐
☐		☐
		☐

i will decompress by:

☐
☐
☐

ending on a good note

3 good things that happened today

Wind Up:

word of the day	date

morning routine	goal for today	tasks
☐		☐
☐		☐
☐		☐
☐		☐
☐		☐
		☐
i will practice self-care by:		☐
		☐

brain dump

what's on your mind?

Wind Down:

i am thankful for

night routine	celebrating myself tonight for	tomorrow's tasks
☐		☐
☐		☐
☐		☐
☐		☐
☐		☐
		☐
i will decompress by:		☐
		☐

ending on a good note
3 good things that happened today

Wind Up:

word of the day	date

morning routine	goal for today	tasks
☐		☐
☐		☐
☐		☐
☐		☐
☐		☐
		☐
i will practice self-care by:		☐
		☐

brain dump
what's on your mind?

_____

_____

_____

_____

_____

_____

_____

_____

_____

_____

_____

Wind Down:

i am thankful for

night routine	celebrating myself tonight for	tomorrow's tasks
☐		☐
☐		☐
☐		☐
☐		☐
☐		☐
		☐

i will decompress by:

☐
☐
☐

ending on a good note

3 good things that happened today

Wind Up:

word of the day	date

morning routine	goal for today	tasks
☐		☐
☐		☐
☐		☐
☐		☐
☐		☐
		☐
i will practice self-care by:		☐
		☐

brain dump

what's on your mind?

Wind Down:

i am thankful for

night routine	celebrating myself tonight for	tomorrow's tasks
☐		☐
☐		☐
☐		☐
☐		☐
☐		☐
		☐
i will decompress by:		☐
		☐

ending on a good note

3 good things that happened today

_____

_____

_____

_____

_____

_____

_____

_____

_____

_____

Wind Up:

word of the day		date

morning routine	goal for today	tasks
☐		☐
☐		☐
☐		☐
☐		☐
☐		☐
		☐
i will practice self-care by:		☐
		☐

brain dump

what's on your mind?

Wind Down:

i am thankful for

night routine	celebrating myself tonight for	tomorrow's tasks
☐		☐
☐		☐
☐		☐
☐		☐
☐		☐
		☐
i will decompress by:		☐
		☐

ending on a good note
3 good things that happened today

_____

_____

_____

_____

_____

_____

_____

_____

_____

Wind Up:

word of the day	date

morning routine	goal for today	tasks
☐		☐
☐		☐
☐		☐
☐		☐
☐		☐
		☐
i will practice self-care by:		☐
		☐

brain dump

what's on your mind?

Wind Down:

i am thankful for

.

night routine	celebrating myself tonight for	tomorrow's tasks
☐		☐
☐		☐
☐		☐
☐		☐
☐		☐
		☐
i will decompress by:		☐
		☐
		☐

ending on a good note

3 good things that happened today

_____

_____

_____

_____

_____

_____

_____

_____

_____

_____

Wind Up:

word of the day		date

morning routine	goal for today	tasks
☐		☐
☐		☐
☐		☐
☐		☐
☐		☐
		☐
i will practice self-care by:		☐
		☐

brain dump
what's on your mind?

_____

_____

_____

_____

_____

_____

_____

_____

_____

_____

Wind Down:

i am thankful for

night routine	celebrating myself tonight for	tomorrow's tasks
☐		☐
☐		☐
☐		☐
☐		☐
☐		☐
		☐
i will decompress by:		☐
		☐

ending on a good note
3 good things that happened today

Wind Up:

word of the day		date

morning routine	goal for today	tasks
☐		☐
☐		☐
☐		☐
☐		☐
☐		☐
		☐
i will practice self-care by:		☐
		☐

brain dump

what's on your mind?

Wind Down:

i am thankful for

night routine	celebrating myself tonight for	tomorrow's tasks
☐		☐
☐		☐
☐		☐
☐		☐
☐		☐
		☐

i will decompress by:

☐
☐
☐

ending on a good note

3 good things that happened today

Wind Up:

word of the day		date

morning routine	goal for today	tasks
☐		☐
☐		☐
☐		☐
☐		☐
☐		☐
		☐
i will practice self-care by:		☐
		☐

brain dump

what's on your mind?

Wind Down:

i am thankful for

night routine	celebrating myself tonight for	tomorrow's tasks
☐		☐
☐		☐
☐		☐
☐		☐
☐		☐
		☐
i will decompress by:		☐
		☐

ending on a good note

3 good things that happened today

Wind Up:

word of the day		date

morning routine	goal for today	tasks
☐		☐
☐		☐
☐		☐
☐		☐
☐		☐
		☐
i will practice self-care by:		☐
		☐

brain dump

what's on your mind?

_____

_____

_____

_____

_____

_____

_____

_____

_____

Wind Down:

i am thankful for

night routine	celebrating myself tonight for	tomorrow's tasks
☐		☐
☐		☐
☐		☐
☐		☐
☐		☐
		☐

i will decompress by:

☐
☐
☐

ending on a good note

3 good things that happened today

_____

_____

_____

_____

_____

_____

_____

_____

_____

Wind Up:

word of the day		date

morning routine	goal for today	tasks
☐		☐
☐		☐
☐		☐
☐		☐
☐		☐
		☐
i will practice self-care by:		☐
		☐

brain dump

what's on your mind?

Wind Down:

i am thankful for

night routine	celebrating myself tonight for	tomorrow's tasks
☐		☐
☐		☐
☐		☐
☐		☐
☐		☐
		☐
i will decompress by:		☐
		☐

ending on a good note

3 good things that happened today

Wind Up:

word of the day		date

morning routine	goal for today	tasks
☐		☐
☐		☐
☐		☐
☐		☐
☐		☐
		☐
i will practice self-care by:		☐
		☐

brain dump

what's on your mind?

Wind Down:

i am thankful for

night routine

- [ ]
- [ ]
- [ ]
- [ ]
- [ ]

celebrating myself tonight for

tomorrow's tasks

- [ ]
- [ ]
- [ ]
- [ ]
- [ ]
- [ ]
- [ ]
- [ ]

i will decompress by:

ending on a good note

3 good things that happened today

Wind Up:

word of the day		date

morning routine	goal for today	tasks
☐		☐
☐		☐
☐		☐
☐		☐
☐		☐
		☐
i will practice self-care by:		☐
		☐

brain dump

what's on your mind?

Wind Down:

i am thankful for

night routine	celebrating myself tonight for	tomorrow's tasks
☐		☐
☐		☐
☐		☐
☐		☐
☐		☐
		☐

i will decompress by:

☐
☐

ending on a good note
3 good things that happened today

Wind Up:

word of the day	date

morning routine	goal for today	tasks
☐		☐
☐		☐
☐		☐
☐		☐
☐		☐
		☐
i will practice self-care by:		☐
		☐

brain dump

what's on your mind?

Wind Down:

i am thankful for		

night routine	celebrating myself tonight for	tomorrow's tasks
☐		☐
☐		☐
☐		☐
☐		☐
☐		☐
		☐
i will decompress by:		☐
		☐

ending on a good note

3 good things that happened today

_____

_____

_____

_____

_____

_____

_____

_____

_____

_____

_____

Wind Up:

word of the day	date

morning routine	goal for today	tasks
☐		☐
☐		☐
☐		☐
☐		☐
☐		☐
		☐
i will practice self-care by:		☐
		☐

brain dump
what's on your mind?

_____

_____

_____

_____

_____

_____

_____

_____

_____

_____

Wind Down:

i am thankful for

night routine	celebrating myself tonight for	tomorrow's tasks
☐		☐
☐		☐
☐		☐
☐		☐
☐		☐
		☐
i will decompress by:		☐
		☐

ending on a good note

3 good things that happened today

Wind Up:

word of the day		date

morning routine	goal for today	tasks
☐		☐
☐		☐
☐		☐
☐		☐
☐		☐
		☐
i will practice self-care by:		☐
		☐

brain dump

what's on your mind?

Wind Down:

i am thankful for

night routine

- [ ]
- [ ]
- [ ]
- [ ]
- [ ]

celebrating myself tonight for

tomorrow's tasks

- [ ]
- [ ]
- [ ]
- [ ]
- [ ]
- [ ]
- [ ]
- [ ]

i will decompress by:

ending on a good note

3 good things that happened today

Wind Up:

word of the day	date

morning routine	goal for today	tasks
☐		☐
☐		☐
☐		☐
☐		☐
☐		☐
		☐
i will practice self-care by:		☐
		☐

brain dump
what's on your mind?

Wind Down:

i am thankful for

night routine	celebrating myself tonight for	tomorrow's tasks
☐		☐
☐		☐
☐		☐
☐		☐
☐		☐
		☐
i will decompress by:		☐
		☐
		☐

ending on a good note
3 good things that happened today

Wind Up:

word of the day	date

morning routine	goal for today	tasks
☐		☐
☐		☐
☐		☐
☐		☐
☐		☐
		☐
i will practice self-care by:		☐
		☐

brain dump

what's on your mind?

_____

_____

_____

_____

_____

_____

_____

_____

_____

_____

_____

Wind Down:

i am thankful for

night routine	celebrating myself tonight for	tomorrow's tasks
☐		☐
☐		☐
☐		☐
☐		☐
☐		☐
		☐
i will decompress by:		☐
		☐

ending on a good note
3 good things that happened today

_____

_____

_____

_____

_____

_____

_____

_____

_____

Wind Up:

word of the day	date

morning routine	goal for today	tasks
☐		☐
☐		☐
☐		☐
☐		☐
☐		☐
		☐
i will practice self-care by:		☐
		☐

brain dump

what's on your mind?

_____

_____

_____

_____

_____

_____

_____

_____

_____

_____

Wind Down:

i am thankful for

night routine	celebrating myself tonight for	tomorrow's tasks
☐		☐
☐		☐
☐		☐
☐		☐
☐		☐

i will decompress by:

☐
☐
☐

ending on a good note
3 good things that happened today

_____
_____
_____
_____
_____
_____
_____
_____
_____
_____

Wind Up:

word of the day		date

morning routine	goal for today	tasks
☐		☐
☐		☐
☐		☐
☐		☐
☐		☐
		☐
i will practice self-care by:		☐
		☐

brain dump

what's on your mind?

Wind Down:

i am thankful for

night routine	celebrating myself tonight for	tomorrow's tasks
☐		☐
☐		☐
☐		☐
☐		☐
☐		☐
		☐
i will decompress by:		☐
		☐

ending on a good note

3 good things that happened today

Wind Up:

word of the day		date

morning routine	goal for today	tasks
☐		☐
☐		☐
☐		☐
☐		☐
☐		☐
		☐
i will practice self-care by:		☐
		☐

brain dump

what's on your mind?

Wind Down:

i am thankful for

night routine	celebrating myself tonight for	tomorrow's tasks
☐		☐
☐		☐
☐		☐
☐		☐
☐		☐
		☐
i will decompress by:		☐
		☐

ending on a good note

3 good things that happened today

Wind Up:

word of the day		date

morning routine	goal for today	tasks
☐		☐
☐		☐
☐		☐
☐		☐
☐		☐
		☐
i will practice self-care by:		☐
		☐

brain dump

what's on your mind?

_____

_____

_____

_____

_____

_____

_____

_____

_____

_____

_____

Wind Down:

i am thankful for

night routine	celebrating myself tonight for	tomorrow's tasks
☐		☐
☐		☐
☐		☐
☐		☐
☐		☐

i will decompress by:

☐
☐
☐

ending on a good note
3 good things that happened today

_____

_____

_____

_____

_____

_____

_____

_____

_____

Wind Up:

word of the day		date

morning routine	goal for today	tasks
☐		☐
☐		☐
☐		☐
☐		☐
☐		☐
		☐
i will practice self-care by:		☐
		☐

brain dump

what's on your mind?

Wind Down:

i am thankful for

night routine	celebrating myself tonight for	tomorrow's tasks
☐		☐
☐		☐
☐		☐
☐		☐
☐		☐
		☐
i will decompress by:		☐
		☐

ending on a good note
3 good things that happened today

Wind Up:

word of the day	date

morning routine	goal for today	tasks
☐		☐
☐		☐
☐		☐
☐		☐
☐		☐
		☐
i will practice self-care by:		☐
		☐

brain dump

what's on your mind?

Wind Down:

i am thankful for

night routine	celebrating myself tonight for	tomorrow's tasks
☐		☐
☐		☐
☐		☐
☐		☐
☐		☐
		☐

i will decompress by:

☐
☐
☐

ending on a good note

3 good things that happened today

_____

_____

_____

_____

_____

_____

_____

_____

_____

Wind Up:

word of the day		date

morning routine	goal for today	tasks
☐		☐
☐		☐
☐		☐
☐		☐
☐		☐
		☐
i will practice self-care by:		☐
		☐

brain dump

what's on your mind?

_____
_____
_____
_____
_____
_____
_____
_____
_____
_____

Wind Down:

i am thankful for

night routine	celebrating myself tonight for	tomorrow's tasks
☐		☐
☐		☐
☐		☐
☐		☐
☐		☐
		☐

i will decompress by:

☐
☐
☐

ending on a good note
3 good things that happened today

Wind Up:

word of the day	date

morning routine	goal for today	tasks
☐		☐
☐		☐
☐		☐
☐		☐
☐		☐
		☐
i will practice self-care by:		☐
		☐

brain dump

what's on your mind?

Wind Down:

i am thankful for

night routine	celebrating myself tonight for	tomorrow's tasks
☐		☐
☐		☐
☐		☐
☐		☐
☐		☐
		☐

i will decompress by:

☐
☐
☐

ending on a good note
3 good things that happened today

_____

_____

_____

_____

_____

_____

_____

_____

_____

_____

_____

Wind Up:

word of the day		date

morning routine	goal for today	tasks
☐		☐
☐		☐
☐		☐
☐		☐
☐		☐
		☐
i will practice self-care by:		☐
		☐

brain dump

what's on your mind?

_____

_____

_____

_____

_____

_____

_____

_____

_____

_____

Wind Down:

i am thankful for

night routine	celebrating myself tonight for	tomorrow's tasks
☐		☐
☐		☐
☐		☐
☐		☐
☐		☐
		☐
i will decompress by:		☐
		☐

ending on a good note

3 good things that happened today

Wind Up:

word of the day		date

morning routine	goal for today	tasks
☐		☐
☐		☐
☐		☐
☐		☐
☐		☐
		☐
i will practice self-care by:		☐
		☐

brain dump

what's on your mind?

Wind Down:

i am thankful for

night routine	celebrating myself tonight for	tomorrow's tasks
☐		☐
☐		☐
☐		☐
☐		☐
☐		☐
		☐
i will decompress by:		☐
		☐

ending on a good note

3 good things that happened today

Wind Up:

word of the day		date

morning routine	goal for today	tasks
☐		☐
☐		☐
☐		☐
☐		☐
☐		☐
		☐
i will practice self-care by:		☐
		☐

brain dump

what's on your mind?

Wind Down:

i am thankful for

night routine	celebrating myself tonight for	tomorrow's tasks
☐		☐
☐		☐
☐		☐
☐		☐
☐		☐
		☐

i will decompress by:

☐
☐

ending on a good note

3 good things that happened today

Wind Up:

word of the day	date

morning routine	goal for today	tasks
☐		☐
☐		☐
☐		☐
☐		☐
☐		☐
		☐
i will practice self-care by:		☐
		☐

brain dump

what's on your mind?

Wind Down:

i am thankful for

night routine	celebrating myself tonight for	tomorrow's tasks
☐		☐
☐		☐
☐		☐
☐		☐
☐		☐
		☐
i will decompress by:		☐
		☐

ending on a good note

3 good things that happened today

Wind Up:

word of the day		date
morning routine	goal for today	tasks

morning routine
☐
☐
☐
☐
☐

goal for today

tasks
☐
☐
☐
☐
☐
☐
☐

i will practice self-care by:

brain dump
what's on your mind?

Wind Down:

i am thankful for

night routine	celebrating myself tonight for	tomorrow's tasks
☐		☐
☐		☐
☐		☐
☐		☐
☐		☐
		☐
i will decompress by:		☐
		☐

ending on a good note
3 good things that happened today

_____

_____

_____

_____

_____

_____

_____

_____

_____

_____

Wind Up:

word of the day	date

morning routine	goal for today	tasks
☐		☐
☐		☐
☐		☐
☐		☐
☐		☐
		☐
i will practice self-care by:		☐
		☐

brain dump

what's on your mind?

_____

_____

_____

_____

_____

_____

_____

_____

_____

_____

Wind Down:

i am thankful for

night routine	celebrating myself tonight for	tomorrow's tasks
☐		☐
☐		☐
☐		☐
☐		☐
☐		☐
		☐
i will decompress by:		☐
		☐

ending on a good note
3 good things that happened today

Wind Up:

word of the day		date

morning routine	goal for today	tasks
☐		☐
☐		☐
☐		☐
☐		☐
☐		☐
		☐
i will practice self-care by:		☐
		☐

brain dump

what's on your mind?

Wind Down:

i am thankful for

night routine	celebrating myself tonight for	tomorrow's tasks
☐		☐
☐		☐
☐		☐
☐		☐
☐		☐
		☐
i will decompress by:		☐
		☐

ending on a good note
3 good things that happened today

Wind Up:

word of the day	date

morning routine	goal for today	tasks
☐		☐
☐		☐
☐		☐
☐		☐
☐		☐
		☐
i will practice self-care by:		☐
		☐

brain dump
what's on your mind?

Wind Down:

i am thankful for

night routine	celebrating myself tonight for	tomorrow's tasks
☐		☐
☐		☐
☐		☐
☐		☐
☐		☐
		☐
i will decompress by:		☐
		☐

ending on a good note
3 good things that happened today

Wind Up:

word of the day	date

morning routine	goal for today	tasks
☐		☐
☐		☐
☐		☐
☐		☐
☐		☐
		☐
i will practice self-care by:		☐
		☐

brain dump

what's on your mind?

Wind Down:

i am thankful for

night routine	celebrating myself tonight for	tomorrow's tasks
☐		☐
☐		☐
☐		☐
☐		☐
☐		☐
		☐
i will decompress by:		☐
		☐

ending on a good note

3 good things that happened today

_____

_____

_____

_____

_____

_____

_____

_____

_____

Wind Up:

word of the day		date

morning routine	goal for today	tasks
☐		☐
☐		☐
☐		☐
☐		☐
☐		☐
		☐
i will practice self-care by:		☐
		☐

brain dump

what's on your mind?

Wind Down:

i am thankful for

night routine	celebrating myself tonight for	tomorrow's tasks
☐		☐
☐		☐
☐		☐
☐		☐
☐		☐
		☐
i will decompress by:		☐
		☐

ending on a good note

3 good things that happened today

Wind Up:

word of the day	date

morning routine	goal for today	tasks
☐		☐
☐		☐
☐		☐
☐		☐
☐		☐
		☐
i will practice self-care by:		☐
		☐

brain dump

what's on your mind?

Wind Down:

i am thankful for

night routine	celebrating myself tonight for	tomorrow's tasks
☐		☐
☐		☐
☐		☐
☐		☐
☐		☐
		☐
i will decompress by:		☐
		☐

ending on a good note

3 good things that happened today

Wind Up:

word of the day	date

morning routine	goal for today	tasks
☐		☐
☐		☐
☐		☐
☐		☐
☐		☐
		☐
i will practice self-care by:		☐
		☐

brain dump

what's on your mind?

_____

_____

_____

_____

_____

_____

_____

_____

_____

_____

_____

_____

Wind Down:

i am thankful for

night routine	celebrating myself tonight for	tomorrow's tasks
☐		☐
☐		☐
☐		☐
☐		☐
☐		☐
		☐
i will decompress by:		☐
		☐

ending on a good note

3 good things that happened today

_____

_____

_____

_____

_____

_____

_____

_____

_____

Wind Up:

word of the day	date

morning routine	goal for today	tasks
☐		☐
☐		☐
☐		☐
☐		☐
☐		☐
		☐
i will practice self-care by:		☐
		☐

brain dump
what's on your mind?

Wind Down:

i am thankful for

night routine	celebrating myself tonight for	tomorrow's tasks
☐		☐
☐		☐
☐		☐
☐		☐
☐		☐
		☐

i will decompress by:

☐
☐

ending on a good note

3 good things that happened today

_____

_____

_____

_____

_____

_____

_____

_____

_____

_____

Wind Up:

word of the day		date

morning routine	goal for today	tasks
☐		☐
☐		☐
☐		☐
☐		☐
☐		☐
		☐
i will practice self-care by:		☐
		☐

brain dump

what's on your mind?

Wind Down:

i am thankful for

night routine	celebrating myself tonight for	tomorrow's tasks
☐		☐
☐		☐
☐		☐
☐		☐
☐		☐
		☐
i will decompress by:		☐
		☐

ending on a good note

3 good things that happened today

Wind Up:

word of the day	date

morning routine	goal for today	tasks
☐		☐
☐		☐
☐		☐
☐		☐
☐		☐
		☐
i will practice self-care by:		☐
		☐

brain dump

what's on your mind?

_____

_____

_____

_____

_____

_____

_____

_____

_____

_____

Wind Down:

i am thankful for

night routine	celebrating myself tonight for	tomorrow's tasks
☐		☐
☐		☐
☐		☐
☐		☐
☐		☐
		☐
i will decompress by:		☐
		☐

ending on a good note

3 good things that happened today

_____

_____

_____

_____

_____

_____

_____

_____

_____

Wind Up:

word of the day	date

morning routine	goal for today	tasks
☐		☐
☐		☐
☐		☐
☐		☐
☐		☐
		☐
i will practice self-care by:		☐
		☐

brain dump

what's on your mind?

Wind Down:

i am thankful for

night routine	celebrating myself tonight for	tomorrow's tasks
☐		☐
☐		☐
☐		☐
☐		☐
☐		☐
		☐
i will decompress by:		☐
		☐

ending on a good note
3 good things that happened today

Wind Up:

word of the day	date

morning routine	goal for today	tasks
☐		☐
☐		☐
☐		☐
☐		☐
☐		☐
		☐
i will practice self-care by:		☐
		☐
		☐

brain dump

what's on your mind?

_____

_____

_____

_____

_____

_____

_____

_____

_____

_____

_____

_____

_____

_____

_____

_____

Wind Down:

i am thankful for		

night routine	celebrating myself tonight for	tomorrow's tasks
☐		☐
☐		☐
☐		☐
☐		☐
☐		☐
i will decompress by:		☐
		☐
		☐

ending on a good note

3 good things that happened today

Wind Up:

word of the day		date

morning routine	goal for today	tasks
☐		☐
☐		☐
☐		☐
☐		☐
☐		☐
		☐
i will practice self-care by:		☐
		☐

brain dump
what's on your mind?

Wind Down:

i am thankful for

night routine	celebrating myself tonight for	tomorrow's tasks
☐		☐
☐		☐
☐		☐
☐		☐
☐		☐
		☐

i will decompress by:

☐
☐
☐

ending on a good note
3 good things that happened today

Wind Up:

word of the day	date

morning routine	goal for today	tasks
☐		☐
☐		☐
☐		☐
☐		☐
☐		☐
i will practice self-care by:		☐
		☐
		☐

brain dump

what's on your mind?

Wind Down:

i am thankful for

night routine	celebrating myself tonight for	tomorrow's tasks
☐		☐
☐		☐
☐		☐
☐		☐
☐		☐
		☐
i will decompress by:		☐
		☐

ending on a good note

3 good things that happened today

Wind Up:

word of the day	date

morning routine	goal for today	tasks
☐		☐
☐		☐
☐		☐
☐		☐
☐		☐
		☐
i will practice self-care by:		☐
		☐

brain dump

what's on your mind?

Wind Down:

i am thankful for

night routine	celebrating myself tonight for	tomorrow's tasks
☐		☐
☐		☐
☐		☐
☐		☐
☐		☐

i will decompress by:

☐
☐
☐

ending on a good note

3 good things that happened today

Wind Up:

word of the day		date

morning routine	goal for today	tasks
☐		☐
☐		☐
☐		☐
☐		☐
☐		☐
		☐
i will practice self-care by:		☐
		☐

brain dump

what's on your mind?

Wind Down:

i am thankful for

night routine	celebrating myself tonight for	tomorrow's tasks
☐		☐
☐		☐
☐		☐
☐		☐
☐		☐
		☐
i will decompress by:		☐
		☐

ending on a good note
3 good things that happened today

Wind Up:

word of the day		date

morning routine	goal for today	tasks
☐		☐
☐		☐
☐		☐
☐		☐
☐		☐
		☐
i will practice self-care by:		☐
		☐

brain dump
what's on your mind?

Wind Down:

i am thankful for

night routine	celebrating myself tonight for	tomorrow's tasks
☐		☐
☐		☐
☐		☐
☐		☐
☐		☐
		☐
i will decompress by:		☐
		☐

ending on a good note
3 good things that happened today

Wind Up:

word of the day		date
morning routine	goal for today	tasks

morning routine
- [ ]
- [ ]
- [ ]
- [ ]
- [ ]

i will practice self-care by:

tasks
- [ ]
- [ ]
- [ ]
- [ ]
- [ ]
- [ ]
- [ ]
- [ ]

brain dump

what's on your mind?

Wind Down:

i am thankful for

night routine	celebrating myself tonight for	tomorrow's tasks
☐		☐
☐		☐
☐		☐
☐		☐
☐		☐
		☐
i will decompress by:		☐
		☐

ending on a good note
3 good things that happened today

Wind Up:

word of the day		date

morning routine	goal for today	tasks
☐		☐
☐		☐
☐		☐
☐		☐
☐		☐
		☐
i will practice self-care by:		☐
		☐

brain dump

what's on your mind?

_____

_____

_____

_____

_____

_____

_____

_____

_____

_____

_____

_____

_____

Wind Down:

i am thankful for

night routine	celebrating myself tonight for	tomorrow's tasks
☐		☐
☐		☐
☐		☐
☐		☐
☐		☐
		☐
i will decompress by:		☐
		☐

ending on a good note

3 good things that happened today

Wind Up:

word of the day		date

morning routine	goal for today	tasks
☐		☐
☐		☐
☐		☐
☐		☐
☐		☐
		☐
i will practice self-care by:		☐
		☐

brain dump

what's on your mind?

Wind Down:

i am thankful for		

night routine	celebrating myself tonight for	tomorrow's tasks
☐		☐
☐		☐
☐		☐
☐		☐
☐		☐
		☐
i will decompress by:		☐
		☐

ending on a good note

3 good things that happened today

Wind Up:

word of the day	date

morning routine	goal for today	tasks
☐		☐
☐		☐
☐		☐
☐		☐
☐		☐
		☐
i will practice self-care by:		☐
		☐

brain dump

what's on your mind?

_____

_____

_____

_____

_____

_____

_____

_____

_____

_____

Wind Down:

i am thankful for

night routine	celebrating myself tonight for	tomorrow's tasks
☐		☐
☐		☐
☐		☐
☐		☐
☐		☐
		☐

i will decompress by:

☐
☐
☐

ending on a good note

3 good things that happened today

Wind Up:

word of the day		date

morning routine	goal for today	tasks
☐		☐
☐		☐
☐		☐
☐		☐
☐		☐
		☐
i will practice self-care by:		☐
		☐

brain dump

what's on your mind?

Wind Down:

i am thankful for

night routine	celebrating myself tonight for	tomorrow's tasks
☐		☐
☐		☐
☐		☐
☐		☐
☐		☐
		☐
i will decompress by:		☐
		☐

ending on a good note

3 good things that happened today

Wind Up:

word of the day		date

morning routine	goal for today	tasks
☐		☐
☐		☐
☐		☐
☐		☐
☐		☐
		☐
i will practice self-care by:		☐
		☐

brain dump

what's on your mind?

Wind Down:

i am thankful for

night routine	celebrating myself tonight for	tomorrow's tasks
☐		☐
☐		☐
☐		☐
☐		☐
☐		☐
		☐
i will decompress by:		☐
		☐

ending on a good note

3 good things that happened today

Wind Up:

word of the day		date

morning routine	goal for today	tasks
☐		☐
☐		☐
☐		☐
☐		☐
☐		☐
		☐
i will practice self-care by:		☐
		☐

brain dump

what's on your mind?

Wind Down:

i am thankful for		

night routine	celebrating myself tonight for	tomorrow's tasks
☐		☐
☐		☐
☐		☐
☐		☐
☐		☐
		☐
i will decompress by:		☐
		☐

ending on a good note

3 good things that happened today

_____

_____

_____

_____

_____

_____

_____

_____

Wind Up:

word of the day	date

morning routine	goal for today	tasks
☐		☐
☐		☐
☐		☐
☐		☐
☐		☐
		☐
i will practice self-care by:		☐
		☐

brain dump

what's on your mind?

Wind Down:

i am thankful for

night routine	celebrating myself tonight for	tomorrow's tasks
☐		☐
☐		☐
☐		☐
☐		☐
☐		☐
		☐
i will decompress by:		☐
		☐

ending on a good note
3 good things that happened today

_____

_____

_____

_____

_____

_____

_____

_____

_____

_____

Wind Up:

word of the day		date
morning routine	goal for today	tasks
☐		☐
☐		☐
☐		☐
☐		☐
☐		☐
		☐
i will practice self-care by:		☐
		☐

brain dump

what's on your mind?

Wind Down:

i am thankful for

night routine	celebrating myself tonight for	tomorrow's tasks
☐		☐
☐		☐
☐		☐
☐		☐
☐		☐
		☐

i will decompress by:

☐
☐

ending on a good note

3 good things that happened today

Wind Up:

word of the day		date

morning routine	goal for today	tasks
☐		☐
☐		☐
☐		☐
☐		☐
☐		☐
		☐
i will practice self-care by:		☐
		☐

brain dump

what's on your mind?

Wind Down:

i am thankful for

night routine	celebrating myself tonight for	tomorrow's tasks
☐		☐
☐		☐
☐		☐
☐		☐
☐		☐
		☐
i will decompress by:		☐
		☐

ending on a good note
3 good things that happened today

_____

_____

_____

_____

_____

_____

_____

_____

_____

_____

Wind Up:

word of the day		date

morning routine	goal for today	tasks
☐		☐
☐		☐
☐		☐
☐		☐
☐		☐
		☐
i will practice self-care by:		☐
		☐

brain dump

what's on your mind?

Wind Down:

i am thankful for

night routine	celebrating myself tonight for	tomorrow's tasks
☐		☐
☐		☐
☐		☐
☐		☐
☐		☐
		☐
i will decompress by:		☐
		☐

ending on a good note
3 good things that happened today

_____

_____

_____

_____

_____

_____

_____

_____

_____

Wind Up:

word of the day		date

morning routine	goal for today	tasks
☐		☐
☐		☐
☐		☐
☐		☐
☐		☐
		☐
i will practice self-care by:		☐
		☐

brain dump

what's on your mind?

Wind Down:

i am thankful for

night routine	celebrating myself tonight for	tomorrow's tasks
☐		☐
☐		☐
☐		☐
☐		☐
☐		☐
		☐

i will decompress by:

☐
☐
☐

ending on a good note
3 good things that happened today

_____

_____

_____

_____

_____

_____

_____

_____

_____

_____

Wind Up:

word of the day		date

morning routine	goal for today	tasks
☐		☐
☐		☐
☐		☐
☐		☐
☐		☐
		☐
i will practice self-care by:		☐
		☐

brain dump
what's on your mind?

Wind Down:

i am thankful for

night routine	celebrating myself tonight for	tomorrow's tasks
☐		☐
☐		☐
☐		☐
☐		☐
☐		☐
		☐
i will decompress by:		☐
		☐

ending on a good note

3 good things that happened today

Wind Up:

word of the day		date

morning routine	goal for today	tasks
☐		☐
☐		☐
☐		☐
☐		☐
☐		☐
		☐
i will practice self-care by:		☐
		☐

brain dump

what's on your mind?

Wind Down:

i am thankful for

night routine	celebrating myself tonight for	tomorrow's tasks
☐		☐
☐		☐
☐		☐
☐		☐
☐		☐
		☐
i will decompress by:		☐
		☐

ending on a good note

3 good things that happened today

_____

_____

_____

_____

_____

_____

_____

_____

_____

Wind Up:

word of the day		date

morning routine	goal for today	tasks
☐		☐
☐		☐
☐		☐
☐		☐
☐		☐
		☐
i will practice self-care by:		☐
		☐

brain dump

what's on your mind?

Wind Down:

i am thankful for

night routine	celebrating myself tonight for	tomorrow's tasks
☐		☐
☐		☐
☐		☐
☐		☐
☐		☐
		☐
i will decompress by:		☐
		☐

ending on a good note

3 good things that happened today

Wind Up:

word of the day		date

morning routine	goal for today	tasks
☐		☐
☐		☐
☐		☐
☐		☐
☐		☐
		☐
i will practice self-care by:		☐
		☐

brain dump

what's on your mind?

Wind Down:

i am thankful for

night routine	celebrating myself tonight for	tomorrow's tasks
☐		☐
☐		☐
☐		☐
☐		☐
☐		☐

i will decompress by:

☐
☐
☐

ending on a good note

3 good things that happened today

Wind Up:

word of the day	date

morning routine	goal for today	tasks
☐		☐
☐		☐
☐		☐
☐		☐
☐		☐
		☐
i will practice self-care by:		☐
		☐
		☐

brain dump
what's on your mind?

Wind Down:

i am thankful for

night routine	celebrating myself tonight for	tomorrow's tasks
☐		☐
☐		☐
☐		☐
☐		☐
☐		☐
		☐

i will decompress by:

☐
☐

ending on a good note
3 good things that happened today

_____
_____
_____
_____
_____
_____
_____
_____
_____
_____
_____

Wind Up:

word of the day	date

morning routine	goal for today	tasks
☐		☐
☐		☐
☐		☐
☐		☐
☐		☐
		☐
i will practice self-care by:		☐
		☐

brain dump

what's on your mind?

_____

_____

_____

_____

_____

_____

_____

_____

_____

_____

Wind Down:

i am thankful for

night routine	celebrating myself tonight for	tomorrow's tasks
☐		☐
☐		☐
☐		☐
☐		☐
☐		☐
		☐

i will decompress by:

☐
☐

ending on a good note
3 good things that happened today

_____

_____

_____

_____

_____

_____

_____

_____

_____

_____

Wind Up:

word of the day		date

morning routine	goal for today	tasks
☐		☐
☐		☐
☐		☐
☐		☐
☐		☐
		☐
i will practice self-care by:		☐
		☐

brain dump

what's on your mind?

Wind Down:

i am thankful for

night routine	celebrating myself tonight for	tomorrow's tasks
☐		☐
☐		☐
☐		☐
☐		☐
☐		☐
		☐

i will decompress by:

☐
☐
☐

ending on a good note
3 good things that happened today

_____

_____

_____

_____

_____

_____

_____

_____

_____

_____

Wind Up:

word of the day	date

morning routine	goal for today	tasks
☐		☐
☐		☐
☐		☐
☐		☐
☐		☐
		☐
i will practice self-care by:		☐
		☐

brain dump

what's on your mind?

Wind Down:

i am thankful for

night routine	celebrating myself tonight for	tomorrow's tasks
☐		☐
☐		☐
☐		☐
☐		☐
☐		☐
		☐
i will decompress by:		☐
		☐

ending on a good note
3 good things that happened today

_____

_____

_____

_____

_____

_____

_____

_____

_____

Wind Up:

word of the day	date

morning routine	goal for today	tasks
☐		☐
☐		☐
☐		☐
☐		☐
☐		☐
		☐
i will practice self-care by:		☐
		☐

brain dump
what's on your mind?

Wind Down:

i am thankful for

night routine	celebrating myself tonight for	tomorrow's tasks
☐		☐
☐		☐
☐		☐
☐		☐
☐		☐
		☐
i will decompress by:		☐
		☐

ending on a good note
3 good things that happened today

Wind Up:

word of the day		date

morning routine	goal for today	tasks
☐		☐
☐		☐
☐		☐
☐		☐
☐		☐
		☐
i will practice self-care by:		☐
		☐

brain dump

what's on your mind?

Wind Down:

i am thankful for

night routine	celebrating myself tonight for	tomorrow's tasks
☐		☐
☐		☐
☐		☐
☐		☐
☐		☐
		☐

i will decompress by:

☐
☐
☐

ending on a good note
3 good things that happened today

_____
_____
_____
_____
_____
_____
_____
_____
_____
_____

Wind Up:

word of the day	date

morning routine	goal for today	tasks
☐		☐
☐		☐
☐		☐
☐		☐
☐		☐
		☐
i will practice self-care by:		☐
		☐

brain dump

what's on your mind?

Wind Down:

i am thankful for

night routine	celebrating myself tonight for	tomorrow's tasks
☐		☐
☐		☐
☐		☐
☐		☐
☐		☐
		☐
i will decompress by:		☐
		☐

ending on a good note
3 good things that happened today

_____

_____

_____

_____

_____

_____

_____

_____

_____

Wind Up:

word of the day	date

morning routine	goal for today	tasks
☐		☐
☐		☐
☐		☐
☐		☐
☐		☐
		☐
i will practice self-care by:		☐
		☐

brain dump

what's on your mind?

_____

_____

_____

_____

_____

_____

_____

_____

_____

Wind Down:

i am thankful for

night routine	celebrating myself tonight for	tomorrow's tasks
☐		☐
☐		☐
☐		☐
☐		☐
☐		☐
		☐
i will decompress by:		☐
		☐

ending on a good note
3 good things that happened today

Wind Up:

word of the day	date

morning routine	goal for today	tasks
☐		☐
☐		☐
☐		☐
☐		☐
☐		☐
		☐
i will practice self-care by:		☐
		☐

brain dump

what's on your mind?

_____

_____

_____

_____

_____

_____

_____

_____

_____

_____

_____

Wind Down:

i am thankful for

night routine	celebrating myself tonight for	tomorrow's tasks
☐		☐
☐		☐
☐		☐
☐		☐
☐		☐
		☐
i will decompress by:		☐
		☐

ending on a good note
3 good things that happened today

Wind Up:

word of the day		date

morning routine	goal for today	tasks
☐		☐
☐		☐
☐		☐
☐		☐
☐		☐
		☐
i will practice self-care by:		☐
		☐

brain dump

what's on your mind?

Wind Down:

i am thankful for

night routine	celebrating myself tonight for	tomorrow's tasks
☐		☐
☐		☐
☐		☐
☐		☐
☐		☐
		☐

i will decompress by:

☐
☐
☐

ending on a good note
3 good things that happened today

_____
_____
_____
_____
_____
_____
_____
_____
_____
_____

Wind Up:

word of the day		date

morning routine	goal for today	tasks
☐		☐
☐		☐
☐		☐
☐		☐
☐		☐
		☐
i will practice self-care by:		☐
		☐

brain dump
what's on your mind?

Wind Down:

i am thankful for

night routine	celebrating myself tonight for	tomorrow's tasks
☐		☐
☐		☐
☐		☐
☐		☐
☐		☐
		☐
i will decompress by:		☐
		☐

ending on a good note
3 good things that happened today

Wind Up:

word of the day	date

morning routine	goal for today	tasks
☐		☐
☐		☐
☐		☐
☐		☐
☐		☐
		☐
i will practice self-care by:		☐
		☐

brain dump

what's on your mind?

Wind Down:

i am thankful for

night routine	celebrating myself tonight for	tomorrow's tasks
☐		☐
☐		☐
☐		☐
☐		☐
☐		☐
		☐

i will decompress by:

☐
☐
☐

ending on a good note

3 good things that happened today

Wind Up:

word of the day		date

morning routine	goal for today	tasks
☐		☐
☐		☐
☐		☐
☐		☐
☐		☐
		☐
i will practice self-care by:		☐
		☐

brain dump

what's on your mind?

Wind Down:

i am thankful for

night routine	celebrating myself tonight for	tomorrow's tasks
☐		☐
☐		☐
☐		☐
☐		☐
☐		☐
		☐
i will decompress by:		☐
		☐

ending on a good note

3 good things that happened today

Wind Up:

word of the day	date

morning routine	goal for today	tasks
☐		☐
☐		☐
☐		☐
☐		☐
☐		☐
		☐
i will practice self-care by:		☐
		☐

brain dump

what's on your mind?

Wind Down:

i am thankful for

night routine	celebrating myself tonight for	tomorrow's tasks
☐		☐
☐		☐
☐		☐
☐		☐
☐		☐
		☐

i will decompress by:

☐
☐
☐

ending on a good note

3 good things that happened today

Wind Up:

word of the day		date

morning routine	goal for today	tasks
☐		☐
☐		☐
☐		☐
☐		☐
☐		☐
		☐
i will practice self-care by:		☐
		☐

brain dump

what's on your mind?

_____

_____

_____

_____

_____

_____

_____

_____

_____

_____

Wind Down:

i am thankful for

night routine	celebrating myself tonight for	tomorrow's tasks
☐		☐
☐		☐
☐		☐
☐		☐
☐		☐
i will decompress by:		☐
		☐
		☐

ending on a good note

3 good things that happened today

Wind Up:

word of the day		date

morning routine	goal for today	tasks
☐		☐
☐		☐
☐		☐
☐		☐
☐		☐
		☐
i will practice self-care by:		☐
		☐
		☐

brain dump

what's on your mind?

Wind Down:

i am thankful for

night routine	celebrating myself tonight for	tomorrow's tasks
☐		☐
☐		☐
☐		☐
☐		☐
☐		☐
		☐
i will decompress by:		☐
		☐

ending on a good note
3 good things that happened today

Wind Up:

word of the day	date

morning routine	goal for today	tasks
☐		☐
☐		☐
☐		☐
☐		☐
☐		☐

i will practice self-care by:

☐
☐
☐

brain dump

what's on your mind?

Wind Down:

i am thankful for

night routine	celebrating myself tonight for	tomorrow's tasks
☐		☐
☐		☐
☐		☐
☐		☐
☐		☐
		☐
i will decompress by:		☐
		☐

ending on a good note
3 good things that happened today

Wind Up:

word of the day	date

morning routine	goal for today	tasks
☐		☐
☐		☐
☐		☐
☐		☐
☐		☐
		☐
i will practice self-care by:		☐
		☐

brain dump
what's on your mind?

Wind Down:

i am thankful for

night routine	celebrating myself tonight for	tomorrow's tasks
☐		☐
☐		☐
☐		☐
☐		☐
☐		☐
		☐

i will decompress by:

☐
☐

ending on a good note

3 good things that happened today

Wind Up:

word of the day		date

morning routine	goal for today	tasks
☐		☐
☐		☐
☐		☐
☐		☐
☐		☐
		☐
i will practice self-care by:		☐
		☐

brain dump

what's on your mind?

_____

_____

_____

_____

_____

_____

_____

_____

_____

_____

_____

Wind Down:

i am thankful for

night routine
- [ ]
- [ ]
- [ ]
- [ ]
- [ ]

celebrating myself tonight for

tomorrow's tasks
- [ ]
- [ ]
- [ ]
- [ ]
- [ ]
- [ ]
- [ ]
- [ ]

i will decompress by:

ending on a good note
3 good things that happened today

Wind Up:

word of the day	date

morning routine	goal for today	tasks
☐		☐
☐		☐
☐		☐
☐		☐
☐		☐
		☐
i will practice self-care by:		☐
		☐

brain dump

what's on your mind?

_____

_____

_____

_____

_____

_____

_____

_____

_____

_____

_____

_____

Wind Down:

i am thankful for

night routine	celebrating myself tonight for	tomorrow's tasks
☐		☐
☐		☐
☐		☐
☐		☐
☐		☐
		☐

i will decompress by:

☐
☐
☐

ending on a good note

3 good things that happened today

Wind Up:

word of the day	date

morning routine	goal for today	tasks
☐		☐
☐		☐
☐		☐
☐		☐
☐		☐
		☐
i will practice self-care by:		☐
		☐
		☐

brain dump

what's on your mind?

Wind Down:

i am thankful for		
night routine	**celebrating myself tonight for**	**tomorrow's tasks**
☐ ☐ ☐ ☐ ☐		☐ ☐ ☐ ☐ ☐ ☐ ☐ ☐
i will decompress by:		

ending on a good note
3 good things that happened today

Wind Up:

word of the day	date

morning routine	goal for today	tasks
☐		☐
☐		☐
☐		☐
☐		☐
☐		☐
		☐
i will practice self-care by:		☐
		☐

brain dump

what's on your mind?

Wind Down:

i am thankful for

night routine	celebrating myself tonight for	tomorrow's tasks
☐		☐
☐		☐
☐		☐
☐		☐
☐		☐
		☐
i will decompress by:		☐
		☐

ending on a good note

3 good things that happened today

Wind Up:

word of the day	date

morning routine	goal for today	tasks
☐		☐
☐		☐
☐		☐
☐		☐
☐		☐
		☐
i will practice self-care by:		☐
		☐

brain dump

what's on your mind?

_____

_____

_____

_____

_____

_____

_____

_____

_____

_____

_____

_____

Wind Down:

i am thankful for

night routine	celebrating myself tonight for	tomorrow's tasks
☐		☐
☐		☐
☐		☐
☐		☐
☐		☐
		☐
i will decompress by:		☐
		☐

ending on a good note
3 good things that happened today

Wind Up:

word of the day		date

morning routine	goal for today	tasks
☐		☐
☐		☐
☐		☐
☐		☐
☐		☐
		☐
i will practice self-care by:		☐
		☐

brain dump

what's on your mind?

Wind Down:

i am thankful for

night routine	celebrating myself tonight for	tomorrow's tasks
☐		☐
☐		☐
☐		☐
☐		☐
☐		☐
		☐
i will decompress by:		☐
		☐

ending on a good note
3 good things that happened today

_____

_____

_____

_____

_____

_____

_____

_____

_____

_____

Wind Up:

word of the day	date

morning routine	goal for today	tasks
☐		☐
☐		☐
☐		☐
☐		☐
☐		☐
		☐
i will practice self-care by:		☐
		☐

brain dump

what's on your mind?

Wind Down:

i am thankful for

night routine	celebrating myself tonight for	tomorrow's tasks
☐		☐
☐		☐
☐		☐
☐		☐
☐		☐
		☐
i will decompress by:		☐
		☐

ending on a good note
3 good things that happened today

Wind Up:

word of the day		date

morning routine	goal for today	tasks
☐		☐
☐		☐
☐		☐
☐		☐
☐		☐
		☐
i will practice self-care by:		☐
		☐

brain dump

what's on your mind?

_____

_____

_____

_____

_____

_____

_____

_____

_____

_____

_____

_____

_____

Wind Down:

i am thankful for

night routine	celebrating myself tonight for	tomorrow's tasks
☐		☐
☐		☐
☐		☐
☐		☐
☐		☐
		☐
i will decompress by:		☐
		☐

ending on a good note

3 good things that happened today

Wind Up:

word of the day		date

morning routine	goal for today	tasks
☐		☐
☐		☐
☐		☐
☐		☐
☐		☐
		☐
i will practice self-care by:		☐
		☐

brain dump

what's on your mind?

_____

_____

_____

_____

_____

_____

_____

_____

_____

_____

_____

Wind Down:

i am thankful for

night routine	celebrating myself tonight for	tomorrow's tasks
☐		☐
☐		☐
☐		☐
☐		☐
☐		☐
		☐
i will decompress by:		☐
		☐

ending on a good note

3 good things that happened today

_____

_____

_____

_____

_____

_____

_____

_____

_____

_____

Wind Up:

| word of the day | date |
| | |

morning routine	goal for today	tasks
☐		☐
☐		☐
☐		☐
☐		☐
☐		☐
		☐
i will practice self-care by:		☐
		☐

brain dump

what's on your mind?

_____

_____

_____

_____

_____

_____

_____

_____

_____

_____

Wind Down:

i am thankful for

night routine	celebrating myself tonight for	tomorrow's tasks
☐		☐
☐		☐
☐		☐
☐		☐
☐		☐
		☐
i will decompress by:		☐
		☐

ending on a good note

3 good things that happened today

_____

_____

_____

_____

_____

_____

_____

_____

_____

_____

Wind Up:

word of the day		date

morning routine	goal for today	tasks
☐		☐
☐		☐
☐		☐
☐		☐
☐		☐
		☐
i will practice self-care by:		☐
		☐

brain dump

what's on your mind?

Wind Down:

i am thankful for

night routine	celebrating myself tonight for	tomorrow's tasks
☐		☐
☐		☐
☐		☐
☐		☐
☐		☐
		☐
i will decompress by:		☐
		☐

ending on a good note

3 good things that happened today

Wind Up:

word of the day	date

morning routine	goal for today	tasks
☐		☐
☐		☐
☐		☐
☐		☐
☐		☐
		☐
i will practice self-care by:		☐
		☐

brain dump

what's on your mind?

_____

_____

_____

_____

_____

_____

_____

_____

_____

_____

_____

Wind Down:

i am thankful for

night routine	celebrating myself tonight for	tomorrow's tasks
☐		☐
☐		☐
☐		☐
☐		☐
☐		☐
		☐
i will decompress by:		☐
		☐

ending on a good note
3 good things that happened today

_____

_____

_____

_____

_____

_____

_____

_____

_____

_____

Wind Up:

word of the day		date

morning routine	goal for today	tasks
☐		☐
☐		☐
☐		☐
☐		☐
☐		☐
		☐
i will practice self-care by:		☐
		☐

brain dump

what's on your mind?

Wind Down:

i am thankful for

night routine	celebrating myself tonight for	tomorrow's tasks
☐		☐
☐		☐
☐		☐
☐		☐
☐		☐
		☐
i will decompress by:		☐
		☐

ending on a good note

3 good things that happened today

Wind Up:

word of the day	date

morning routine	goal for today	tasks
☐		☐
☐		☐
☐		☐
☐		☐
☐		☐

i will practice self-care by:

☐
☐
☐

brain dump
what's on your mind?

_____

_____

_____

_____

_____

_____

_____

_____

_____

_____

Wind Down:

i am thankful for

night routine	celebrating myself tonight for	tomorrow's tasks
☐		☐
☐		☐
☐		☐
☐		☐
☐		☐
		☐
i will decompress by:		☐
		☐

ending on a good note
3 good things that happened today

_____

_____

_____

_____

_____

_____

_____

_____

_____

_____

Wind Up:

word of the day		date

morning routine	goal for today	tasks
☐		☐
☐		☐
☐		☐
☐		☐
☐		☐
		☐
i will practice self-care by:		☐
		☐

brain dump

what's on your mind?

Wind Down:

i am thankful for

night routine	celebrating myself tonight for	tomorrow's tasks
☐		☐
☐		☐
☐		☐
☐		☐
☐		☐

i will decompress by:

☐
☐
☐

ending on a good note

3 good things that happened today

Wind Up:

word of the day		date

morning routine	goal for today	tasks
☐		☐
☐		☐
☐		☐
☐		☐
☐		☐
		☐
i will practice self-care by:		☐
		☐
		☐

brain dump

what's on your mind?

Wind Down:

i am thankful for

night routine	celebrating myself tonight for	tomorrow's tasks
☐		☐
☐		☐
☐		☐
☐		☐
☐		☐
		☐

i will decompress by:

☐
☐
☐

ending on a good note

3 good things that happened today

Wind Up:

word of the day		date

morning routine	goal for today	tasks
☐		☐
☐		☐
☐		☐
☐		☐
☐		☐
		☐
i will practice self-care by:		☐
		☐

brain dump
what's on your mind?

Wind Down:

i am thankful for

night routine	celebrating myself tonight for	tomorrow's tasks
☐		☐
☐		☐
☐		☐
☐		☐
☐		☐
		☐

i will decompress by:

☐
☐

ending on a good note
3 good things that happened today

Wind Up:

word of the day		date

morning routine	goal for today	tasks
☐		☐
☐		☐
☐		☐
☐		☐
☐		☐
		☐
i will practice self-care by:		☐
		☐

brain dump

what's on your mind?

_____

_____

_____

_____

_____

_____

_____

_____

_____

_____

_____

Wind Down:

i am thankful for

night routine	celebrating myself tonight for	tomorrow's tasks
☐		☐
☐		☐
☐		☐
☐		☐
☐		☐

i will decompress by:

☐
☐
☐

ending on a good note

3 good things that happened today

_____
_____
_____
_____
_____
_____
_____
_____
_____

Wind Up:

word of the day		date

morning routine	goal for today	tasks
☐		☐
☐		☐
☐		☐
☐		☐
☐		☐
		☐
i will practice self-care by:		☐
		☐

brain dump

what's on your mind?

_____

_____

_____

_____

_____

_____

_____

_____

_____

_____

_____

Wind Down:

i am thankful for

night routine	celebrating myself tonight for	tomorrow's tasks
☐		☐
☐		☐
☐		☐
☐		☐
☐		☐
		☐
i will decompress by:		☐
		☐

ending on a good note

3 good things that happened today

Wind Up:

word of the day		date

morning routine	goal for today	tasks
☐		☐
☐		☐
☐		☐
☐		☐
☐		☐
		☐
i will practice self-care by:		☐
		☐

brain dump

what's on your mind?

_____
_____
_____
_____
_____
_____
_____
_____
_____
_____
_____
_____

Wind Down:

i am thankful for

night routine	celebrating myself tonight for	tomorrow's tasks
☐		☐
☐		☐
☐		☐
☐		☐
☐		☐
		☐
i will decompress by:		☐
		☐

ending on a good note

3 good things that happened today

Wind Up:

word of the day		date

morning routine	goal for today	tasks
☐		☐
☐		☐
☐		☐
☐		☐
☐		☐
		☐
i will practice self-care by:		☐
		☐

brain dump

what's on your mind?

_____

_____

_____

_____

_____

_____

_____

_____

_____

_____

Wind Down:

i am thankful for

night routine	celebrating myself tonight for	tomorrow's tasks
☐		☐
☐		☐
☐		☐
☐		☐
☐		☐
		☐
i will decompress by:		☐
		☐

ending on a good note

3 good things that happened today

Wind Up:

word of the day	date

morning routine	goal for today	tasks
☐		☐
☐		☐
☐		☐
☐		☐
☐		☐
		☐
i will practice self-care by:		☐
		☐

brain dump

what's on your mind?

Wind Down:

i am thankful for

night routine
- [ ]
- [ ]
- [ ]
- [ ]
- [ ]

celebrating myself tonight for

tomorrow's tasks
- [ ]
- [ ]
- [ ]
- [ ]
- [ ]
- [ ]
- [ ]
- [ ]

i will decompress by:

ending on a good note
3 good things that happened today

Wind Up:

word of the day	date

morning routine	goal for today	tasks
☐		☐
☐		☐
☐		☐
☐		☐
☐		☐
i will practice self-care by:		☐
		☐
		☐

brain dump

what's on your mind?

Wind Down:

i am thankful for

night routine	celebrating myself tonight for	tomorrow's tasks
☐		☐
☐		☐
☐		☐
☐		☐
☐		☐
		☐
i will decompress by:		☐
		☐

ending on a good note

3 good things that happened today

_____

_____

_____

_____

_____

_____

_____

_____

_____

_____

Wind Up:

word of the day		date

morning routine	goal for today	tasks
☐		☐
☐		☐
☐		☐
☐		☐
☐		☐
		☐
i will practice self-care by:		☐
		☐

brain dump

what's on your mind?

Wind Down:

i am thankful for

night routine
- [ ]
- [ ]
- [ ]
- [ ]
- [ ]

celebrating myself tonight for

tomorrow's tasks
- [ ]
- [ ]
- [ ]
- [ ]
- [ ]
- [ ]
- [ ]
- [ ]

i will decompress by:

ending on a good note

3 good things that happened today

Wind Up:

word of the day	date

morning routine	goal for today	tasks
☐		☐
☐		☐
☐		☐
☐		☐
☐		☐
		☐
i will practice self-care by:		☐
		☐

brain dump

what's on your mind?

Wind Down:

i am thankful for

night routine	celebrating myself tonight for	tomorrow's tasks
☐		☐
☐		☐
☐		☐
☐		☐
☐		☐
		☐
i will decompress by:		☐
		☐

ending on a good note
3 good things that happened today

Wind Up:

word of the day		date

morning routine	goal for today	tasks
☐		☐
☐		☐
☐		☐
☐		☐
☐		☐
		☐
i will practice self-care by:		☐
		☐

brain dump

what's on your mind?

Wind Down:

i am thankful for

night routine	celebrating myself tonight for	tomorrow's tasks
☐		☐
☐		☐
☐		☐
☐		☐
☐		☐
		☐
i will decompress by:		☐
		☐

ending on a good note
3 good things that happened today

_____
_____
_____
_____
_____
_____
_____
_____
_____
_____
_____

Wind Up:

word of the day		date

morning routine	goal for today	tasks
☐		☐
☐		☐
☐		☐
☐		☐
☐		☐
		☐
i will practice self-care by:		☐
		☐

brain dump
what's on your mind?

_____

_____

_____

_____

_____

_____

_____

_____

_____

_____

Wind Down:

i am thankful for

night routine	**celebrating myself tonight for**	**tomorrow's tasks**
☐		☐
☐		☐
☐		☐
☐		☐
☐		☐
		☐
i will decompress by:		☐
		☐

ending on a good note

3 good things that happened today

_____

_____

_____

_____

_____

_____

_____

_____

_____

_____

Wind Up:

word of the day		date

morning routine	goal for today	tasks
☐		☐
☐		☐
☐		☐
☐		☐
☐		☐
		☐
i will practice self-care by:		☐
		☐
		☐

brain dump

what's on your mind?

Wind Down:

i am thankful for

night routine	celebrating myself tonight for	tomorrow's tasks
☐		☐
☐		☐
☐		☐
☐		☐
☐		☐
		☐
i will decompress by:		☐
		☐

ending on a good note
3 good things that happened today

_____

_____

_____

_____

_____

_____

_____

_____

_____

_____

_____

_____

Wind Up:

word of the day	date

morning routine	goal for today	tasks
☐		☐
☐		☐
☐		☐
☐		☐
☐		☐
		☐
i will practice self-care by:		☐
		☐

brain dump

what's on your mind?

Wind Down:

i am thankful for

night routine	celebrating myself tonight for	tomorrow's tasks
☐		☐
☐		☐
☐		☐
☐		☐
☐		☐
		☐
i will decompress by:		☐
		☐

ending on a good note

3 good things that happened today

Wind Up:

word of the day	date

morning routine	goal for today	tasks
☐		☐
☐		☐
☐		☐
☐		☐
☐		☐
		☐
i will practice self-care by:		☐
		☐

brain dump

what's on your mind?

Wind Down:

i am thankful for

night routine	celebrating myself tonight for	tomorrow's tasks
☐		☐
☐		☐
☐		☐
☐		☐
☐		☐

i will decompress by:

☐
☐
☐

ending on a good note
3 good things that happened today

Wind Up:

word of the day	date

morning routine	goal for today	tasks
☐		☐
☐		☐
☐		☐
☐		☐
☐		☐
		☐
i will practice self-care by:		☐
		☐

brain dump

what's on your mind?

_____

_____

_____

_____

_____

_____

_____

_____

_____

_____

Wind Down:

i am thankful for

night routine	celebrating myself tonight for	tomorrow's tasks
☐		☐
☐		☐
☐		☐
☐		☐
☐		☐
		☐
i will decompress by:		☐
		☐

ending on a good note

3 good things that happened today

_____

_____

_____

_____

_____

_____

_____

_____

_____

_____

Wind Up:

word of the day	date

morning routine	goal for today	tasks
☐		☐
☐		☐
☐		☐
☐		☐
☐		☐
		☐
i will practice self-care by:		☐
		☐

brain dump

what's on your mind?

_____

_____

_____

_____

_____

_____

_____

_____

_____

_____

Wind Down:

i am thankful for

night routine	celebrating myself tonight for	tomorrow's tasks
☐		☐
☐		☐
☐		☐
☐		☐
☐		☐

i will decompress by:

☐
☐
☐

ending on a good note

3 good things that happened today

Wind Up:

word of the day		date

morning routine	goal for today	tasks
☐		☐
☐		☐
☐		☐
☐		☐
☐		☐
		☐
i will practice self-care by:		☐
		☐
		☐

brain dump

what's on your mind?

Wind Down:

i am thankful for

night routine	celebrating myself tonight for	tomorrow's tasks
☐		☐
☐		☐
☐		☐
☐		☐
☐		☐

i will decompress by:

☐
☐
☐

ending on a good note

3 good things that happened today

Wind Up:

word of the day	date

morning routine	goal for today	tasks
☐		☐
☐		☐
☐		☐
☐		☐
☐		☐
		☐
i will practice self-care by:		☐
		☐

brain dump

what's on your mind?

Wind Down:

i am thankful for

night routine	celebrating myself tonight for	tomorrow's tasks
☐		☐
☐		☐
☐		☐
☐		☐
☐		☐
		☐
i will decompress by:		☐
		☐

ending on a good note

3 good things that happened today

Wind Up:

word of the day	date

morning routine	goal for today	tasks
☐		☐
☐		☐
☐		☐
☐		☐
☐		☐
		☐
i will practice self-care by:		☐
		☐

brain dump

what's on your mind?

Wind Down:

i am thankful for

night routine	celebrating myself tonight for	tomorrow's tasks
☐		☐
☐		☐
☐		☐
☐		☐
☐		☐
		☐

i will decompress by:

☐
☐

ending on a good note
3 good things that happened today

_____

_____

_____

_____

_____

_____

_____

_____

Wind Up:

word of the day		date

morning routine	goal for today	tasks
☐		☐
☐		☐
☐		☐
☐		☐
☐		☐
		☐
i will practice self-care by:		☐
		☐

brain dump

what's on your mind?

_____

_____

_____

_____

_____

_____

_____

_____

_____

_____

Wind Down:

i am thankful for

night routine

- [ ]
- [ ]
- [ ]
- [ ]
- [ ]

celebrating myself tonight for

tomorrow's tasks

- [ ]
- [ ]
- [ ]
- [ ]
- [ ]
- [ ]
- [ ]
- [ ]

i will decompress by:

ending on a good note

3 good things that happened today

Made in the USA
San Bernardino, CA
08 July 2020